The Science of Energy

LIVING SCIENCE

Sarah Dann

Gareth Stevens Publishing
MILWAUKEE

For a free color catalog describing Gareth Stevens' list of high-quality books and multimedia programs, call 1-800-542-2595 (USA) or 1-800-461-9120 (Canada). Gareth Stevens Publishing's Fax: (414) 225-0377.

Library of Congress Cataloging-in-Publication Data available upon request from publisher. Fax (414) 225-0377 for the attention of the Publishing Records Department.

ISBN 0-8368-2571-3 (lib. bdg.)

This edition first published in 2000 by
Gareth Stevens Publishing
1555 North RiverCenter Drive, Suite 201
Milwaukee, WI 53212 USA

Project Co-ordinator: Meaghan Craven
Copy Editors: Marg Cook, Rennay Craats, and Colleen Shantz
Design and Illustration: Warren Clark
Cover Design: Carole Knox
Layout: Lucinda Cage
Gareth Stevens Editor: Rita Reitci

Every reasonable effort has been made to trace ownership and to obtain permission to reprint copyright material. The publishers would be pleased to have any errors or omissions brought to their attention so that they may be corrected in subsequent printings.

Photograph Credits:
BC Hydro: page 10 right; Corel Corporation: pages 4 left, 5 top, 5 left center, 7 center, 9 left, 9 top right, 9 top right top, 9 bottom right, 10 left, 11, 14 bottom, 16 right, 21, 23 bottom, 29 top, 30 bottom, 31;Rob Curle: pages 26 bottom; Eyewire: pages 6, 7 left, 7 right, 8, 14 top, 16 left; GM Media: page 28 bottom; Kristen Higgens: pages 18, 19; Ivy Images: pages 4 right, 24 top; National Biodiesel Board: page 29 bottom; Ontario Science Center: page 22; Sorcha McGinnis: page 20 bottom; Photodisc: cover, pages 13, 15 top, 30 top; Colleen Shantz: page 9 bottom right center; Tom Stack: pages 12 top (Brian Parker), 15 bottom (J. Lotter), 17 right (Dave Watts), 23 top (Wm. L. Wantland), 27 bottom (Thomas Kitchin); Visuals Unlimited: pages 5 left, 5 right center, 5 right, 12 bottom (Arthur R. Hill), 17 left (M. Rashid), 20 top (Steve McCutcheon), 24 bottom (Mark S. Skalny), 25 center, 25 top (Richard L. Carlton), 26 top, 27 top, 28 top (Bruce Gaylord).

Printed in Canada

1 2 3 4 5 6 7 8 9 04 03 02 01 00

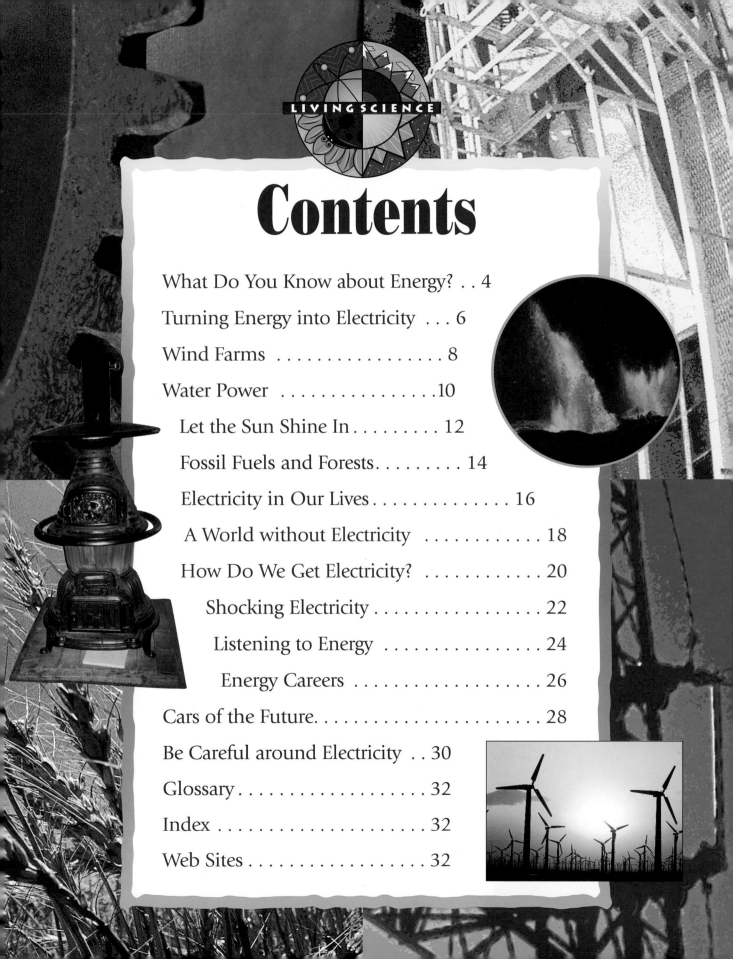

Contents

What Do You Know about Energy?

Energy is the force, or power, to do work. Work happens when an object is moved.

Energy comes in many forms. Wind, water, light, and heat are forms of energy. When energy moves or changes, we call it **kinetic energy**. When energy stays still or is being stored, we call it **potential energy**. It can be used in the future.

The Sun is an important source of energy, called **solar** energy.

Kinetic energy passes from your arm to the pool cue when you make a shot. The ball receives kinetic energy when it is hit by the cue.

The Sun provides energy for all life on Earth. Plants use the energy of sunlight to change a part of the air we breathe, called **carbon dioxide**, into water and sugar. The sugar is then stored in the plants as a source of energy. If an animal eats a plant, the plant's stored energy passes to the animal. Animals receive their energy by eating plants or other animals. This series of steps is called an energy chain.

Activity

Make an Energy Chain

Create an energy chain for a farm animal. Begin with the Sun.

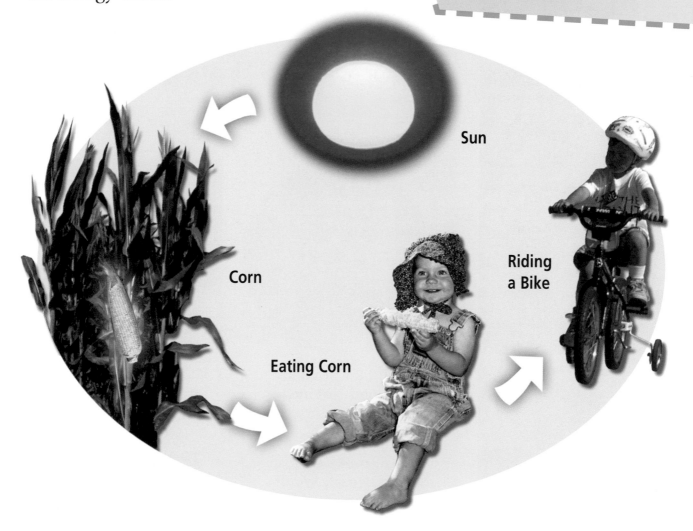

Sun

Corn

Eating Corn

Riding a Bike

The Sun's rays give the corn plants energy to grow. When people eat corn, their bodies obtain the energy necessary for certain activities, such as riding a bicycle.

Turning Energy into Electricity

People have found ways to turn the energy in wind, water, light, and fire into **electricity**. Electricity is produced using inventions including windmills and water **dams**. We use these energy sources to heat and light our homes and run appliances, such as refrigerators.

Different Sources of Electricity

Wind

- Blowing air or wind turns wind turbines and moves sailboats.

- Wind power can be used to make electricity. Strong, steady winds are needed for this power system.

- Wind power does not pollute.

Water

- Water falling from a high place to a low place creates kinetic energy.

- Most water power is used to make electricity.

- Water power does not pollute.

Puzzler

Sometimes your family's car may feel hot when you first get into it in the summer. Do you know why this happens?

Answer: If the car is sitting outside in the sunshine, the Sun's rays pass through the glass windows. The car traps the heat from the Sun inside where it cannot escape.

Solar/Sun	Fossil Fuels	Nuclear

- Sunshine can be captured using glass panels and other solar inventions.

- The Sun's energy can be changed into electricity or heat.

- Solar power does not pollute.

- The major **fossil fuels** are coal, natural gas, and petroleum.

- Petroleum is used to make gasoline, diesel, and heating fuels. It fuels machines that produce electricity.

- Fossil fuels pollute.

- **Nuclear energy** is released by changes in **atoms**. Everything in the universe is made up of atoms.

- Heat from nuclear energy can make electricity.

- Nuclear energy pollutes.

Wind Farms

Wind can be used to create electricity. Wind farms are areas supporting anywhere from three to hundreds of wind turbines. Wind turbines use the wind's energy to run **generators**. Generators are machines that change wind power into electrical energy.

The blowing wind turns propellers that spin the turbine. The spinning turbine runs the generator that produces electricity. The more the wind blows and the faster the blades turn, the more electricity can be produced.

Using wind to make electricity is pollution-free. Some people think this energy source will be used more in the future.

Wind farms need to be in areas where the wind blows without stopping. Prairies and other flat lands are good places for wind farms. People are planning to set up wind farms in the middle of the ocean. Oceans are good places for wind farms because there are no objects like mountains to block the wind.

Wind farms can cause some problems. Birds may be hurt when they come into contact with wind turbines.

The flat desert land in Arizona is good for wind farms.

Puzzler

Which of the following locations would be best for a wind farm?

a forest

an orchard

a small valley

a prairie

Answer: a prairie.

Water Power

Water is an important source of energy. People build dams across rivers to force the water to flow through turbines. Turbines have giant fan blades. Water spins the blades, which turn a generator to make electricity. The kinetic energy of water has been changed into electrical energy.

California's Oroville Dam, the tallest in the United States, uses flowing water to run generators. These generators turn the power of the water into electricity.

Dams can damage the river environment. When a dam is built, fish cannot travel up and down the river. A dam can trap too much water. This causes flooding that kills plants and animals living nearby.

People who live near rivers sometimes have to move when dams are built. Changing the flow of the river often floods homes in the area.

Flooding can happen when a dam is first built. Once the dam is in place, it can help stop floods by limiting the amount of water in the river.

Activity

Do Some Research

You can begin to understand how a dam works by doing this activity.

1. Have an adult help you use scissors to cut the bottom off an empty plastic bottle.
2. Leave the cap on the bottle.
3. Turn the bottle upside-down and fill it with water.
4. Now unscrew the cap.

See how the water pushes out of the small hole in the bottle. This is what happens when river water is forced through turbines in a dam.

Let the Sun Shine In

Sunshine can also be used to make electricity. This process is known as solar power generation. Solar means coming from the Sun. Panels made of a material called silicon change light energy into electrical energy.

Solar panels are made up of hundreds of small containers, or **cells**, that collect and store the Sun's energy.

People who depend on solar energy need to have sunlight year-round.

Many people who use solar power are concerned about the environment. They like solar power because it is the cleanest source of energy. Other people use solar power because they live far away from large cities. Solar power is the only source of electricity available to them.

Solar power plants are being built to provide electricity for companies.

Puzzler

Imagine the appliances in your house run on solar power. What can block the supply of electricity?

Answer:
Your answer might include: cloudy days, short winter days, or snow and leaves trapped on the solar panels.

Fossil Fuels and Forests

Gas, coal, and oil are common sources of energy that are called fossil fuels. They come from the remains of plants and animals buried deep underground millions of years ago. Fossil fuels, such as gasoline, give off heat when they burn. They are used to power many things. Once they are used up, they are gone forever.

Gasoline burns in our cars when we drive. The gas that results is harmful to the environment and our health.

Wood from forests is another source of energy for some people. It is also used to build homes and make paper. Forest areas are being cut down all over the world because of the great need for wood.

There are many ways to help save our wood and fossil fuel resources. Dropping old school notebooks into recycling bins is one method. New paper goods can be made from old ones.

Walking or bicycling to school saves energy because these activities do not use gasoline.

Activity

Be Aware
How much paper do you use every week? Ask your family to place all the paper they use during one week into a box. At the end of the week, gather your family together and view the results. Discuss how you can use less paper. Whether or not your family recycles, using less is always best.

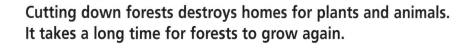

Cutting down forests destroys homes for plants and animals. It takes a long time for forests to grow again.

Electricity in Our Lives

People in North America use a lot of electrical energy every day. It is one of the most common forms of energy. Electrical energy is used to run our factories, computers, lights, televisions, refrigerators, and other appliances.

Keeping lights on in high-rise buildings for hours at a time takes a lot of energy.

Many people in the world do not have electricity. Some people cannot afford to buy it. Others live in countries that are not prepared to supply electricity. These people use **traditional** methods to live, such as cooking their food over an open fire.

Instead of using water wells with electric pumps, some people walk for miles to rivers and bring the water to their homes by foot.

People in some countries use fire to cook their meals and keep warm.

Puzzler

Which of the following items do not need electricity to run?
- a candle
- a computer
- a grand piano
- a light bulb
- a microwave oven

Answer: Neither a candle nor a grand piano need electricity to run.

A World without Electricity

When settlers first came to North America, they lived without electricity. Imagine a day without the use of electricity.

Oil lamps
were used before there were electric lights. The lamps burned an oil called kerosene to create light.

Wood stoves
can become very hot from the burning wood inside. People once used wood stoves for cooking and for heating their homes. A lot of wood had to be cut and dried for burning during the winter.

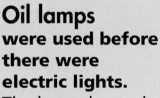

Pumping water
by hand takes a lot of work. Before electric pumps, people had to use hand pumps to take water from wells.

Washing machines were very different before electricity.

Imagine having to scrub every piece of clothing, rinse it, and then wring it out. Then you would have to hang everything out to dry.

Butter is not easy to make without electricity.

People used butter churns to stir cream and salt until it became thick enough to make butter.

Not everyone owned a washing machine.

Before electricity, most people only had scrub boards, wash tubs, and clothes lines. Washing clothes by hand took more time and effort than using washing machines.

Activity

Time Yourself

Try spending a few hours every day for one week without using electrical energy. Write down what you do and how long it takes. Do you spend more time doing regular tasks when you do not use electric tools?

How Do We Get Electricity?

The type of electricity we use in our homes is called **current electricity**. Current electricity comes from generators. Generators are machines that produce almost all of the electricity used by people. They run on energy sources like coal. Energy from burning fuel turns water into steam to spin the fan blades of a turbine generator. The generator changes kinetic energy into electrical energy.

Coal is taken up from underground and piled on the surface. Generators, like the one below, often use coal to produce electricity.

Electricity moves from generators through large wire cables to houses and businesses. **Electricians** then connect smaller wires in houses to the large wires to bring electrical energy into homes. When you plug an appliance into a wall **outlet** or flip on a switch, you tap into the flow of current electricity.

Electric current runs through power lines to reach houses and businesses. This string of wires allows you to turn on a lamp!

Activity

Search for Outlets

How many electrical outlets do you have in your house? Count them. Look in every room. Are there any rooms that have no electrical outlets?

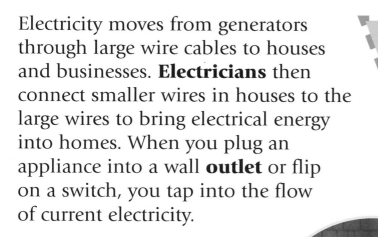

Shocking Electricity

Have you ever taken off a sweater and had it cling to your hair? Or shuffled across the carpet in your socks, touched someone, and experienced a shock? These are two examples of **static electricity**. Static electricity is energy that builds up on the surface of an object.

A Van de Graaff generator produces a high electrical charge. If you touch it, your hair stands straight up on end!

Lightning is the most awesome example of static electricity. Water droplets inside storm clouds bump into one another. Each time they bump, some of their kinetic energy changes into electrical energy. The electrical energy builds up as static electricity. Lightning is the electrical energy moving from cloud to cloud or from the clouds to the ground.

During a lightning storm, lightning is most likely to hit tall things like trees and sailboats. Staying inside during lightning storms is the safest thing to do.

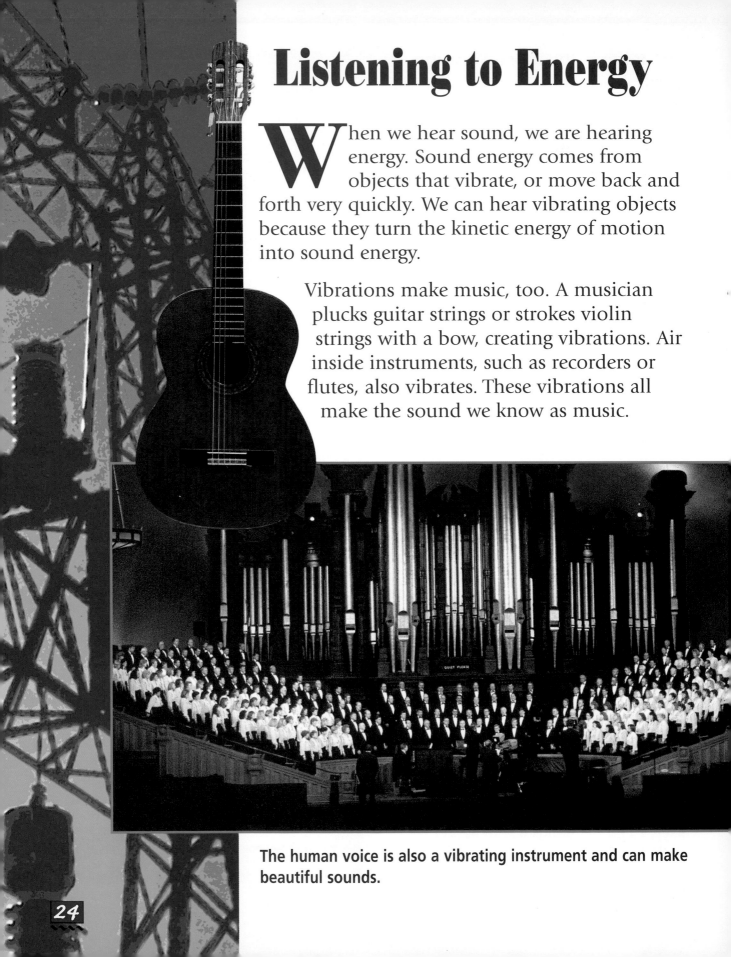

Listening to Energy

When we hear sound, we are hearing energy. Sound energy comes from objects that vibrate, or move back and forth very quickly. We can hear vibrating objects because they turn the kinetic energy of motion into sound energy.

Vibrations make music, too. A musician plucks guitar strings or strokes violin strings with a bow, creating vibrations. Air inside instruments, such as recorders or flutes, also vibrates. These vibrations all make the sound we know as music.

The human voice is also a vibrating instrument and can make beautiful sounds.

The sounds we hear in nature are also created by vibrations. A lightning bolt expands air quickly. This sends a vibration through the air. We hear its energy as the rumbling sound of thunder. We see lightning before we hear it because light travels faster than sound.

The loudest sound in nature is the sound of a volcano erupting.

Puzzler

Describe the sounds made by:
a) taking off a sweater that has static
b) hitting a baseball with a bat
c) turning on a computer
d) running a fan

Answer:
Your answers might include such descriptive words as: crackle, crack, click, and hum.

Energy Careers

Many people work with **natural energy resources**. These are the energy sources we take from Earth. They include trees, coal, water, oil, and gas.

There are many oil and gas careers. Coal miners work underground. They dig coal out of the ground. It can be a dangerous job. Roughnecks are members of drilling crews. They operate drills that find oil and gas below the ground.

Miners wear lights on their hats to see the coal underground. Roughnecks drill for oil on land and at sea.

Trees are an important source of energy. Forest managers work with trees. They help people use trees wisely. They also make sure forests are replaced.

Some scientists study tree diseases and find new ways to keep trees healthy.

Tree planters work to replace trees that have been cut down.

Puzzler

How many careers focus on supplying people with energy? Make a list. Compare it to the list below.

Answer: Dam operator, electrician, electrical engineer, mechanic, miner, and tree planter are just a few examples.

Cars of the Future

Cars use a great amount of energy. They need gasoline and oil to run. These fossil fuels create pollution when they burn. People are working on designing cars that use cleaner energy sources.

Electric cars exist today. They are much cleaner than cars that burn gasoline and oil. Electric cars do not have a power cord attached. They run on **battery** power.

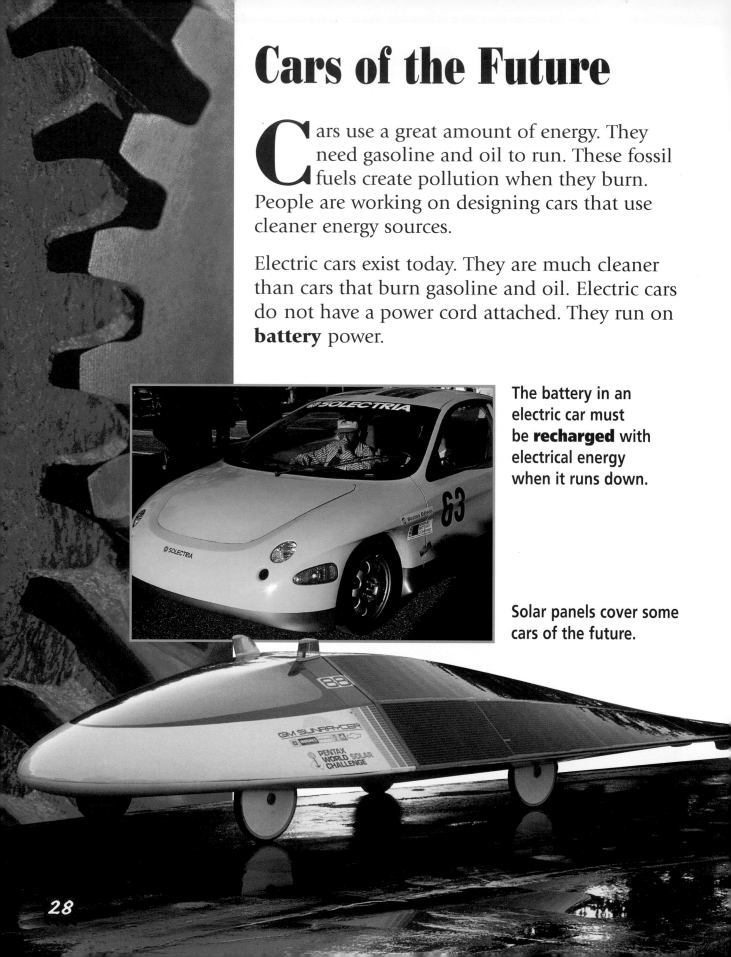

The battery in an electric car must be **recharged** with electrical energy when it runs down.

Solar panels cover some cars of the future.

Vegetable oil is another possible energy source. Vegetable oil burns more cleanly than fossil fuels. One car running on vegetable oil traveled 10,000 miles (16,000 km) in 1997. Its exhaust smelled like french fries!

Activity

Invent a Car

Invent your own car of the future. What does it look like? What is its source of energy? Maybe it runs on food power! Draw it.

A vehicle run on vegetable oil or soybeans would help the environment. These fuel sources can be replanted and grown again.

SOYBEAN POWERED
This Bus Runs On Soybean Bio-Diesel

54

This Bus Gets 250 Miles Per Acre.

Be Careful around Electricity

Electricity is dangerous if it is not used properly. For example, if a person touches current electricity, it will burn him or her. People must be careful when they use electricity.

There are wires behind the electrical outlets in your walls. They carry electric current into your home. When an appliance is plugged into the outlet, electric current flows into the appliance. Electricity provides energy to the appliance to make it work.

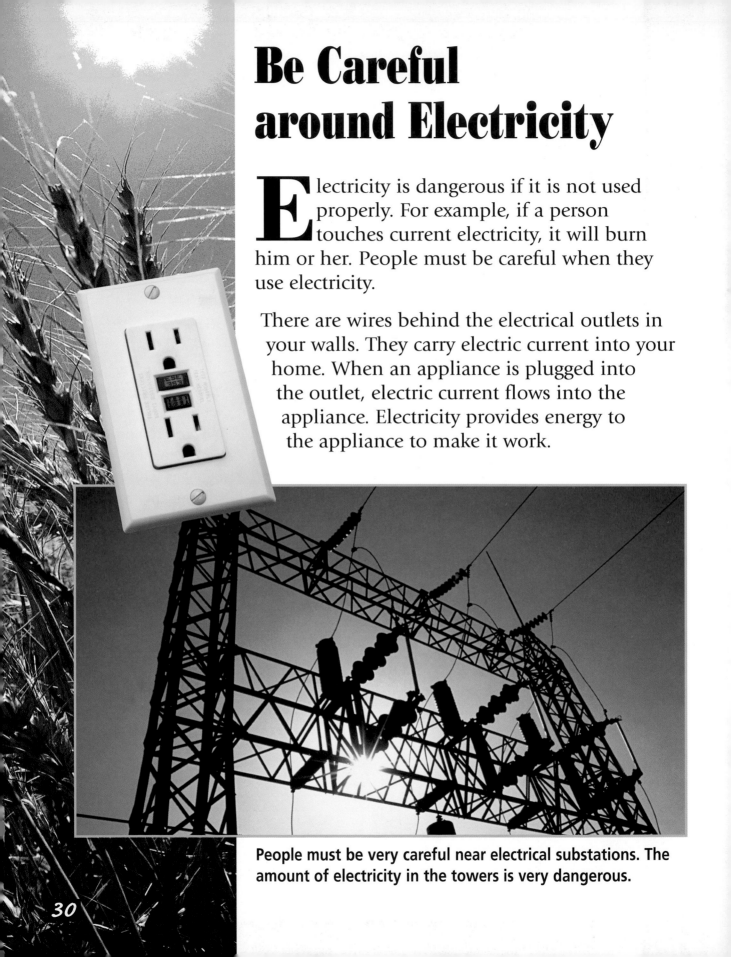

People must be very careful near electrical substations. The amount of electricity in the towers is very dangerous.

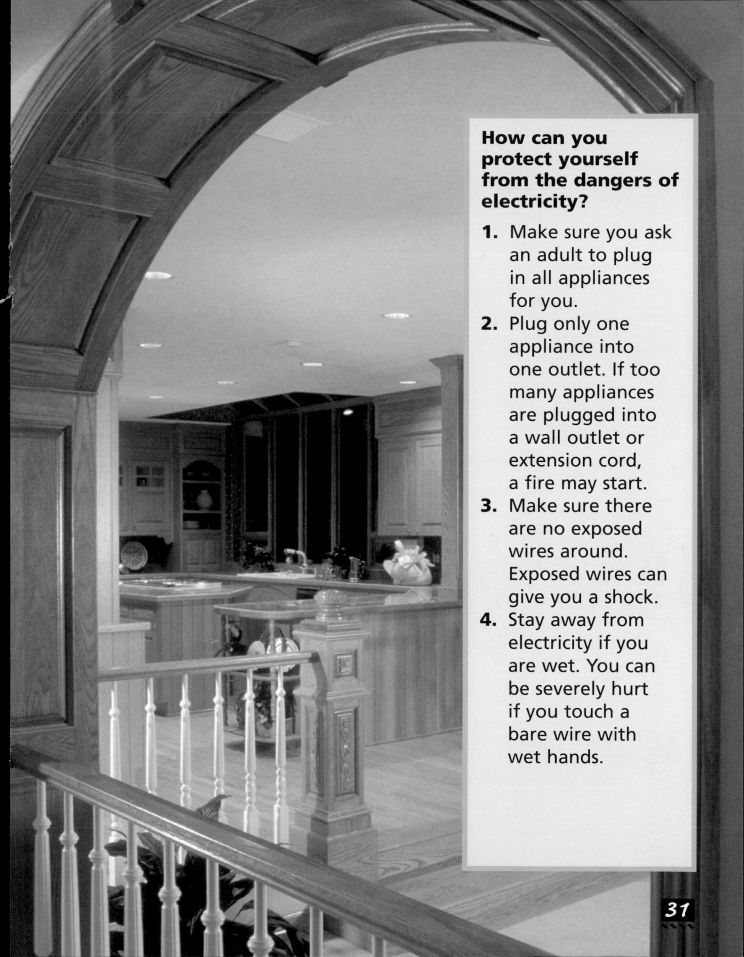

How can you protect yourself from the dangers of electricity?

1. Make sure you ask an adult to plug in all appliances for you.

2. Plug only one appliance into one outlet. If too many appliances are plugged into a wall outlet or extension cord, a fire may start.

3. Make sure there are no exposed wires around. Exposed wires can give you a shock.

4. Stay away from electricity if you are wet. You can be severely hurt if you touch a bare wire with wet hands.

Glossary

atoms: tiny particles that make up all matter in the universe.

battery: a container holding materials that produce electrical energy.

carbon dioxide: a heavy gas present in the air.

cell: a small container.

current electricity: electricity or energy running through wires.

dams: walls built to hold back flowing water.

electrician: a person trained to work with electricity.

electricity: a basic form of energy produced by generators.

fossil fuels: the remains of plants and animals used as energy sources.

generators: machines that produce electricity from different energy sources, such as wind, water, fossil fuels, and the Sun.

kinetic energy: the energy of movement.

natural energy resources: energy sources taken from the Earth.

nuclear energy: energy that is released from atoms.

outlet: a place in a wall where electric current can be accessed.

potential energy: stored energy.

recharge: to charge with energy again.

solar: coming from the Sun.

static electricity: energy that builds up on the surface of an object.

traditional: something that has been done the same way for a long time.

Index

Web Sites

www.edisonkids.com/heroexb/thomas.htm

www.surfnetkids.com/wind.htm

volcano.und.nodak.edu/vwdocs/kids.html

tqjunior.advanced.org/6064/

Some web sites stay current longer than others. For further web sites, use your search engines to locate the following topics: *battery, fossil fuels, mining, natural gas, solar energy,* and *sugar.*